Oh One Arrow——published by **flim forum press**——po box 549, slingerlands, ny 12159——www.flimforum.com——**flim forum press** is + Oh One Arrow edited by: matthew klane + adam golaski——cover/insert art: luke daly——design: jeremy withers printed by: boyd printing co., albany, ny——ISBN 978-0-9790888-0-3——Oh One Arrow copyright——© 2007 by: **flim forum press**, all rights reserved, poems copyright © by our authors——**flim forum press**——

Oh One Arrow

from **the Alps**

Brandon Shimoda

the Alps

alternating   between the green

breast   lateral languages

less invented than   colored

tailed-as nearly   the entire schist

confidentially   with the ribs of the horse

to bind the phoric in one   spirit

harrowing   to work

an emptied mask

and emboldened magic pricks   among the ears

the Alps

with the force of gravity   the trammel of flanks

swooping bergs moving deeply   through

the ambulant stacks   the scratching

throat   calling endlessly upon the dell

warm grappa to awaken   ill-possessing

the demon bears'   to climb a ways through

ovations of bougainvillea   maundering

                            grasses bending their blue

dicks famous five gloves   out-killing

the Alps

malodorous   with 20 – 40 raw eyelets

selected ropes   unhanded

to see the sun

fan the height of

mt. fortune willing   its inheritors

illuminated   in a naked lack

                    the bladders increase the glenning

no black emerged   from the stand

pea-arks the obstacles   but the laughter

the Alps

from a yodel   comes a man to his taste

eyes behind him transitioning   the hay

freed from an extended battery   unetched

thorn sallow silvery   orange on stone

installing his slab on the side of the stable for us

             in order to find her

unsure of saying yes to the formulating Japanese

an irresistible top   imprisoned

amongst the agreement   lowing to calm

the Alps

find your inheritance   strung

                                                             among aprons

caught in blood elder   and the madame used

to say   within the sleeves of a stolen manteau

                              in wide indiscretionary measures

along the cross   rucked

over devaluing eves   take this needle

into yourself   the modellistica earth

eroding into nation-blanknessess sort   of

the Alps

from stones   loosened in the hills the province reel

bags of spumous stones   hisses of ag

in the fables women long   heavy on their saddles

tender voices coming across   the shoulders

of the stricken lords   rectifying

what   had   been thought merrily filled   with smoke

or trying   nuptial garlands unwelcoming

to the weak   the fat communicating

                                purple   purple hood

the Alps

fibrous in their fallows   the covers remove

the crudes marionetting the crudes   on consoles

in the test of the eye   converting

                           out the uninfluences

ulterior to the tonal mountain

without movement   blows empty in the lake

dispersing over the knee and not   simply

the sapphire thread   the lilac

field   defective flowers small along their inner part

the Alps

in the outside the delicate white   the dark

cream-colored and able   youth

given the model   to squander

in search of a history   indiscreet priests

poke at curled limbs   afloat   in the plaza fountains

                              a yellow noise insteadies a red

                                        with married women

are the case with travelers to crook   a rich

dialect   strongly industrialized

the Alps

hazel   a genuine haunt between limit and field

white untiring air   the dipper of white

in degree with the bodies   unloaded

endearingly onto the cobblestones   inter-earth

                                        for the arms

meat but for the blue   in the previous periods

gotten a part of what alarms   the new transition

enabling overweight children   to arrive

without shame from the wool-   pleated runs

the Alps

torrent crimson cliffs go well   into the wood

between the center and the cross

                              on the other side Italian land

laying siege and bent upon the other   side

                        to thine enemy barrow overtipped

q: are they worse   than mountains

a: part of the earth touches   the sky

envoys soaring in the air   barbatus

of the last known death   from the mouth

the Alps

s'alt Wyb

                        comes the dame to a lamentable end

lambs carrying away a three-year old

                            walking in a glen watching

on a wing would be so wild to cross the coast

the Alps

                                embrace / embrace

the fearful look in your hazel eyes

                     the rabbit hardly the alpine brown

returns to its ptarmigan covey

                        hardly the plumage to winter

Devotion 1
Devotion 2
Devotion 3
Devotion 5

Thom Donovan

Devotion 1

Slow the birds showing pulse flocks

             Locus of power but reversed

The name we share a dispersion
                    to what effect.

             The name we share

Slow the birds showing pulse flocks

Owe or words   shower else

Lower aria   poll flows

Over-head, low   how pulse shook

Owe less stock
Owe ease shock
Vase sh
As
We risk address
We re-stack
Windows
Tow to endow

Slowed hold hold hold flocks of
flocks of slowed hold hold

                    hold hold slow birds of flocks
                          of

                            cathect

Registration drive this most simple
division

the motor of the heart of the motor

Devotion 2

To know
if you can know

the flat portraiture
rectangle necessary

irrevocable memoir
of when we were not separable

Windmills stalk flat flat flat flat

all wind blown at wind push weather

push all mill wind through color the wash

the reeds of a plain and

flat the wind pushed through them

Towering in its gesture
their simple relay
like machines do

The wind conveyed
by points that flutter
drawn by wash

Flat cross asymmetric make aerial

make conveyance make
courses through winds graves

flat cross
the mark from an aerial
my sole blank bird

my flat vanished arrow
by cursor pushing which way

What more endemic but wind?

weeds
reeds weeds reeds
weeds reeds
weeds

blank of a cross
pure reed simple move

smooth cloth
smooth cloth
cloth smoothed

What the child looks at while it has vision
of having a flower before its mind
and the flower
the flower holding her
face and breast

mute the start.
The child gazing beyond
The colors of the flower

vibration and eyes deep

If we were young child and
the face young and honest

depersonalized upon
a fold of your hand
clasping
some object

the brushstrokes would show this

With flesh contact

canvas   gaze at

a slight bend over which we call landscape

not flatness, not merely time

to the horizon

world
where it begins and ends

Slight bud and bend swell
and blood obsess

alabaster, spirits
equation for making weather
sound as weather does

expansion through it and without
to a cold stretch of green gray land

the cheek to show me my own soft watch

Devotion 3

Being beside
other days humans

separate the flesh mass

thunder being beside
suddenly this fence

Sand
an impossible
waterway line

instinct
move for
phenomenal tuft

indiscriminate
a point to
a distance ahead

a distance ahead
a way

On the backs points and
desert tongue

reel from sweet music
memory of orgy

artillery in a distance
without history

madness
without joyful test

Test of truth
league of wish
for infinity
sight of flight

savagery
from the photograph of work

there the ink

the screen my thought of it
while it is spilling

would be dark

We cried in games
bad air pact
bird in sub-state (substrates)
places where none march straight

we beat the graves
and covered earth with sound
of the real like a dark stone
between two dark stones

Pray for me too…

from nothing but distance
is each night born

where a mile is not a mile
where a sun's not a sun

capitalize this refusal

Not the kids
the wrap-around dead

pushed up by car
to ladder

to him

Pushed up   put guns
down   words
hostage to light

dear deer above
scrape the dust

(more often the place we return to)

…small machines
deer redeemed from context

caption:
to none aimed in fog

Near enough to nearly touch
their fingers, their lapels

women and men in black
sign and small world
preposition is our silence

The eye in the cat's body

flashes

the face
an animal's intention

if sickness were grace

Where vision is removed the human

Where vision is replaced our thoughts tend

**Devotion 5
"Karbala on their lips"**

The "human wave
attacks"

represented

the most
disturbing

and gruesome
parade

of mass self-
sacrifice

in

living

memory comparable

only to
battles

at Flanders during

the First World War
in which

tens of thousands

of men were hounded

from
their trenches

into

the firing range of the newly

developed machine guns in

the seventy
years since

no officers

or army leaders had been
willing to pay

such an
inconceivable
price

for such tiny territorial
gains

the most striking
thing about

the Iranian
"human
wave attacks"

however
was the degree

of readiness to die

it caused

Iraqi machine

gunners to flee

not only because

they ran out
of

ammunition

but also because they were driven

almost mad because

they could no longer bear

to shoot children
the same
age as their own

until the 1979
revolution

these children

grew up just
like
children

anywhere
else poor

perhaps not
entirely happy but

all the same

with a profound
sense that it was better

to be alive
than

dead now

they
were

rushing to

their deaths as if
the world

had been

turned upside

down

and it was always
the same
word Karbala

Karbala

on their lips

Karbala

on their flags

All words from Christopher Reuter's *My Life is a Weapon* (Princeton University Press, 2004).

The Byzantine Jar
Lazarus, the lucky, the generous

Jonathan Minton

The Byzantine Jar

1.)

A history begins as in
time "in its irresistible and ceaseless flow,"
as in routine migrations, as in some measure of their events,
whether by foot, by wing, or weather, the weather
routinely disrupts the passage, as in time of flood,
when riverbanks, no longer marginal,
gather what will be written as scenarios of decline

in which was named "Peter"
and called "Peter the Hermit,"
having suffered at the hands of Saracens

    (with sheets of undyed linen cut into strips
    (and crosses over their shoulders, the women and children
    (who had left their countries for travel
    (who craved only reality, but could not stomach it
    (who did not believe, trading their own lives for stories

        —this is the texture of voice: that
        —is the translation of arrival

(Their arrival
(did not take place at the same moment
(nor by the same road

____

The historian places one of thirteen
never-decorated Hedwig beakers

        (unfinished "blank"
        ("miraculous glass"

which bears likeness to Islamic objects of rock crystal

which would have been decorated with green lions, eagles, griffins

which should have held water turned to wine as St. Hedwig drank

which may have traveled from Jerusalem to Belarus
from Belarus to Burgandy
according to chemical analysis

which will be labeled as
partial foreign gesture.

2.)

What call you then verbs of gesture?
Verbs of moving, going, resting or doing?

As in "to follow" after "might have been," as in
the migratory lines of flight still evident
even in the absence of birds, or to place an object in view

of the kitchen window, after which a hand gestures
from the window to dark wood,
to the absence of green,
to ink where the page was blank.

(The green returns as Hedwig glass
(Returns as eagle over green seascape
(Returns as something still chemical clinging to the window

____

There is no object, says the historian,
which seeing you, cannot claim you.
No window to a place without placement,
no placement without naming, no naming
without gesturing, as in the way a hand
holds forth its jar of birdseed.

Lazarus, the lucky, the generous

For years after, he followed the migratory habits of birds, tracking, for instance, a family of flammulated owls to South America, where he kept a record of their distinct facial markings: rufous edges that varied in color from burgundy, to brown, to dull rust. He collected prehistoric ceramics and inscribed each fragment with a word from his personal codex: *bibayin* for red, *reybak* for bright but broken. In a basket made from wicker and camel hair, he kept letters from his sisters, their unsent replies written on cocoon paper harvested from marona trees. He never learned the native words for the local insects, so he called each variety *piloa*—after the pending *papalotl*, the pupae—thinking it the most fortunate of creatures. Otherwise, he kept silent and took care to labor no more than a sparrow's measure. When in abundance, he ate maize and lime, scattering what was left for the parrots that arrived each morning. In seasons of drought, he dressed in festival robes, looked to the east for signs of rain, and carefully noted the temperature each time an egret unsettled its reedbed and took flight—the same as when he first emerged from his tomb, his arms extended, with one hand pointing beyond the crowd to an empty space in the grass, the other holding a single white feather.

Voice Notes 1: Three Horses
Voice Notes 2: Rt. Two-Hundred Dead
Voice Notes 4: Back and Forth on 84

Adam Golaski

Voice Notes 1: Three Horses

Voice Notes) 8:22 — 8:44am

My drive describes a route

two-hundred.

Wed. morning
grin'nd grip
wheel

glad t'be en route'nd
t'see th'light th'light
change

week to week each week

a new climb

to brightness.

East

nine'd eas-t'two-hundred
eas-t'two-hundred
eas-t'two-hundred two-hundred'nd two mountains
t'travel two-hundred ramp t'two-hundred'nd
Take ramp t'two-hundred'nd I'm eager to see

You to travel t'two-hundred to Town | Pump'a
double-tanker turns t'two-hundred Bonner: two
Milltown at junction t'two-ten take two-hundred
gas station is video store Take two-hundred,
it's Yours, Butte: one-twelve too Take two-hundred t'two-
hundred'nd ice-curve'nd

curve   light.

Flat light.

Above th'mountains'a
hand'v light
I went t'th'car
alone'nd
th'railroad signal-lights
were illuminated in th'sun
only illuminated in th'sun.

A cold glow
th'low coolant light'a
flat light'a line'v light'a
curv'across th'sky
t'sand-light ice-light broken mill bursting w/ wood
chip spray wood dust'nd white light lost orange flat-light
t'headlight white'nd th'river cover'd w/ ice
Who holds the icy steering wheel the icy field?
I'm eager t'see You out here You ice covered
river an ice-mist rises from th'river steam'nd
th'arm'v a log-lifter clean white steam in th'
background an orange hood an'orange hat'nd one half-a gallon'v gas this morning's snow light blue
blank't'v pale light'nd low-coolant light trees'r dusted snow'nd glow Can you hear my voice? Ov'r

rumble My mind wanders to th'rumble strip'a horse on'its flank frozen'another stands stock still
stands stock'ina frozen field'a frozen bowl th'mountains'another horse kicks'a frozen
metal bowl a bowl fill'd w/ frozen water'nd bitter air three horses see an invisible
angle a curve across invisible ground three horses see a sword drawn.

People and

So Balaam said to Balak

stock still'nd frozen
horses' voices

"Let me pray on this."

Voice Notes) 12:00 – 12:29pm

When the horses speak
their languag'is
invisible.

West

tractor trailer turns'out
Bonner   Missoula
town pipe two-hundred t'Take town pipe two-hundred
two rivers t'two rivers bank accelerate Take
full note ramp creek t'two-hundred blue streak'v jet
stream cattle cut through th'field thin ice th'cattle

water through th'field through Marlborough: $four thirty-
six two-ten'nd railroad x-ing t'two hundred
Take two-hundred'nd two mountains cattle cut
through ice-wall'nd stand still stock still frozen water
from green grain-feeder
from black water-tower
t'broken mill bursting.

A finger-wagging log
leads me along lumber truck'nd
felled trees How did I dip down into snow country?
Water flag hammer'd t'log truck's draft draws me left
toward frozen field'nd cattle draws m'left t'ward three
horses:

th'tree that
looks
th'wires'v'a
human brain

eye itchy icy ground Take t'frozen icy ground cattle cut the icy ground'nd chomp th'frozen
field. Three horses voices language invisible. My itchy eye o'er You in Your classroom th'mule
brays'an unused horse-gate gravel spittle windshield accelerate ina car I fidget not move
nine'd miles per hour o'er two hundred this is how'I Take two-hundred I do not move You do not
move a horse frozen on its flank another stock still stands stock still ina frozen field another
kicks'nd bursts pulls'nd Takes o'er an invisible angle stands in th'road w/ sword drawn th'frozen
field only cattle'nd frozen grass grass gone ice-green'nd ice-orange'nd two mountains third horse
calls invisible

throat-sore from teaching You
'nd learning what's'n empty spaces
what's'n frozen fields
frozen grass'nd
grazing cattle

I see

frozen grass'nd
grazing cattle

three horses th'rocks as if they'd been brushed up red
bushes'nd rocks w/ golden coats Will mountain goats
b'gather'd by the side'v th'road? Three horses
lumber rumbles'away th'cattle'r gather'd
between two trees. How heat ripples the air icy
air. Balaam, how many horses should I offer
to the alter? Fence posts'nd traffic three horses
lead. A truck pulls w/'t a cloud of white dust its
cargo   dust

th'lumber rumbles away.

Voice Notes 2: Rt. Two-Hundred Dead

Voice Notes) 3/16 — 4/21/2005

Dead

rt. two-hundred

raven raccoon corpse
light feather raven wing
ebon feather ebon eye
rings'v ebon   feather'nd

beak rings'v lit gray
tip black crown bone beak'nd
river raven'nd river
ebon feather ebon'ey

black feet   dessicate
rt. two-hundred raccoon
rt. two-hundred th' clutch'nd
closure raven'nd river

rt. two-hundred'a
stiff'nd steaming river
runs'a
long
correspondence:
rt.'nd river   raven'nd

th'clutch'nd closure
th'fog lights highlight'a
rt.'nd black luminous snout
five fluorescent pallbearers

repair th'guardrail
where bent white bouquet where
blue bouquet'nd white cross   mist
th'monument'v white'nd

blue bouquet where light
th'call'v gray mountains
mist   corpse'v monument'nd
long call'v rt. two-hundred.

You should know I
if I could go back
I'd change
You know I
I remove myself
You
waver
ever collective
fluc-
You at one'at two
waver ever You   You,

unreliable reader.

In'n

          in'n other landscape no less real
          in'n'other landscape nonetheless
          in'n'other landscape no th'unless real
          there:

blue ants swarm
up   dead

this'other landscape interferes itself upon
this landscape

beset th'dead w/'a knot
ant swarm'n'a deadly
mill   ring w/'n th'cubicles'v'a corpse
body   typesetter's
box swarm'n ink ants

read:

eow, iow, yeau, heou heow, how, yehw, eou
yeu, yew, ou, hou, zu, iou, aeu, ew,
heu, eo, oea, howe yeow, yuw, ov, ow,
owe, youe, yiu, eu, yu, iow, yuu, yhow
yow, yowe, yoow, yw, yo, yewe, yhu,   You

emerges

blue ants'a brand
up   dead'nd
rotting
flower at night
eyes th'size'v'a slow crawl
across

You   face
earnest
read tree tops

          rt. two-hundred

You
deer
blood b'hind Yr'ear.
black'ey'd'nd blank'a
horse gazes o'er th'dead

12:02pm
center
th'landscape
12:04pm
shadow'o'er wake: n'insect caught th'grill
12:07pm
three living rams get'out
tak'a picture
12:08pm
a living hors'at th'dead deer
carcass You
change from living
t'dead from one t'collected
You change
united.

12:12
Adorning th'yard th'metal silhouett'v'a living animal
cold stove shaped lik'a living animal
12:07
examine th'wire barrier get'out
'nd tak'a picture.

1:27
A horse gaz'o'er th'dead
1:29
eyes swarm'o'er th'dead
1:31
shifting
mass'v identity: one vs. whole
1:17
thriving: You
collective
one   course.

Voice Notes 4: Back and Forth on 84

good,

morning

th'lights
all

all morning
th'lights

flickered

all faded
th'lights
all faded
dust

dust-yellow faded
flickered

all,

black

exhausted

th'lights

exhausted

I met'em all
faded
dust-yellow
mornings,

newspapers,

blown across th'highway

On'a bedsheet
filthy w/
exhaust
"Welcome Home Jeffrey Fox"

See th'moon behind me almost full but

faded

gray-made valley filled w/ fog

roadway rivulet
deer ina ditch
all
clambr'nd crow
all

observation,
coffin,
automobile

Rain five days drive in the rain
rain five days driv'n the rain
rain five days driv'n'th'rain
rain five days drivn rain rain
five days drivn rain rain fiv'
day drivn rain rain fiv day
drivn rain rain'v day drivn
rain rainv day drivn rain rain
day drivn ra'n ra'n day drivn
ran ran day drivn ran
ran d'y drivn ran ran d'y
dr'vn ran ran dy dr'vn
r'n r'n dy drvn r'n r'n dy
dr'n rn rn'dy dr'n rn
dr dyd r dyd r dyd

rain five days still no sky
at'll

five days'v rain
on th'way
t'th'hospital

on th'way t'th'hospital'nd back

again

bladed and milk-muddied clouds drag green along w/ white but blue gray cups
riding in th'spray ov'a Roadway Express truck

th'thick gray whorl'v gray white clouds
bred shape from the little valley

As storm clears'a way people gather'd t'clap
Granddad,
I can't tell th'clouds from th'hills high gray hills'nd low gray clouds

rained five days drive'n th'spray
exhaust

options:

Th'music's mostly gray w/ red points'v light
The air + rain is mostly sky'nd rain w/ deer'nd broken line
Mine'nd mine t'see
The day is mostly flooded road w/ brake lights'nd rain
the mist + rain is mostly autos w/ autos autos autos'nd hands
Granddad,
The flooded road is mostly air w/ hands
objects'v
the air + rain mostly sky'nd rain w/ deer
look!

Th'coffins of th'broken sky

    drive

        exhaust

a cross
"there can be a white cross"
a white cross w/
"Jesus Saves"
drawn upon

a man stands
perpetual
horizontal
rain
rain'nd spray
rain + exhaust
up on a white cross

a man stands in the breakdown lane + we say,
"what we shall be has not yet been revealed"
w/'a cross a white cross + the phrase
"Jesus Saves" drawn across

drawn upon

exhaust

"[   ] open wide"
"[   ] the music"
"[   ] of your task"

        [laughs]

destination:

as th'road is
repaired
signs'r covered

black

black plastic fabric
drawn'nd covered

all arrows'r
covered

84 North
+
South

Back
+
Forth

My trembling auto
smashed

+ ashes

Lori Anderson Moseman

All Steel, Self-Dump Rake[1906]

"The very best testimonials are too often sold as a first-class tool…

Each [who] spoke
                built on suspension
                                widely staggered
                        flanged by a nut
                                        on each side

wheeling
        making connection
                casting form bearing for the dump…

Is this not worth something to you?   …   Hold the teeth up

        to the highest
                point for heavy bunching.
                                        Drop quickly.

See, no unraked muck behind the windrow.

                                T[h]rills brought close together.
        This is the surest and simplest method in use."

                        Speed of harvest will have you

        long for spring's harrowing.

[1906] Use with No. 6 Reaper: "It does not follow that because all Reapers look pretty much alike, and all certainly will cut grain, that they are of equal use to the farmer." See catalogue for details: Adriance, Platt & Company's *American Harvesting Machinery* (Poughkeepsie, New York: 1906).

Labor Pool: First Tool

2nd wave [1978

axe—the first tool we're issued on site
then, a rusty file to sharpen our blade
steel on forged steel—a skinned knee

we stroke unidirectional to the edge
drought hills our brittle California gold
we whittle underbrush arbutus strung out

we whack all day & boys stalk our thighs
count out militia songs hurl insults
until we swing a labyris their way

backlash [2004

cane—the first tool we're issued at home
the one granddaddy broke to poke his boar
tap tap tap we girls with our champion gilts

move them slow in front of the judge slap
the jowls the front quarter bruising shows up
on white pigs on a Hampshire's white stripe

(that thin beauty queen sash on a shoulder
roast) future farmers we parade market hogs
for the joy of slop and being singled out

Protestant Ladder]   [Catholic Ladder

Spaulding[1842] makes Paul quite small,]   [De Smet[1843] tweaks his Bishop's chart.

all denim blue and to the right of Jesus.]   [Etchings inch up: Eden (left) = eternity/

Later, up her path—her vertical strut—]   [hell (right); then, Babel (left), Ark (right);

a little Luther lectures to tinier folks.]   [Moses (l) / Sodom (r). Prophets (l) / kings (r).

Besides that, it's just empty space up]   [Mary & her manger loom larger than any

right to apex angel(s) in sugarplum blue.]   [station of the cross. Her kid's halfway up.

Up left's axis, outsizing the crucified,]   [Then demigods tick off territory and list

a Pope, belted black robe by a river]   [heretics in the vein pattern of poison oak.

of blood, then three fires—each one]   [40 years after Shining Shirt's vision,

hotter/higher 'til Pontiff is upside down,]   [Salish boys (with pick axes, Peavy poles,

suspended above hell. Her wall hanging]   [T-squares & saws) pose[1880] on the roof

for Nez Perce. No rungs connect the two]   [of St. Ignatius Boy's Workshop. So armed,

struts up. Impassable. Unlike the map]   [they can build a cage just as grand as this.

Twisted Hair[1805] made Clark on elk skin.]   [(*in my Father's house are many rooms*[1 BC])

[1842] Using inks and berry dyes, Eliza Spaulding made a proselytizing chart to contest the Catholic Ladder created by Bishop Blanchet in 1838. Eliza's husband, Reverend Henry Spalding, was the first Presbyterian missionary to the Nez Perce. *Sacred Encounters* (U of Oklahoma Press, 1993:110-111).

[1843] Lured by a *shared sacred calendar with sacred colors, sensorially rich rituals, transporting prayers* (+ prophecy by their medicine man Shining Shirt), Salish sought out Black Robes. They got Father Pierre-Jean De Smet of Belgium who "sailed for America in 1821, secreted out of Amsterdam along with eight other would-be Jesuits." *Sacred Encounters* (U of Oklahoma Press, 1993:23,27).

[1880] "On entering with others he has to keep silent until he can speak English.... Such boys as are able should alternately learn reading & writing & some trade." Caption juxtaposed with the photo in *Sacred Encounters* (U of Oklahoma Press, 1993:144-145).

[1805] Twisted Hair, Nez Perce Chief, mapped the river systems flowing west into the Columbia for Lewis and Clark's expedition on white elk skin (Ambrose, Stephen E. *Undaunted Courage*, NY: Simon & Schuster, 1996:299).

[1 BC] John 14:1-2

Homemaking Myth: House

1964 | 2004

the neighborhood is without lariat   [911 hang-up

note fenceline][ ][ ][ ][ ][]   how a posse starts   ] surveillance

1000 store-bought   [[over-the-fence
            Barbie clothes   cop's binocs
                        silk appaloosa   SEE   skin-n-bones
pinto pinto plastic pinto

we play with her stuff
        'til she gets a real horse

                                          [][] home-schooled pubescence

        stable gentry stucco temporarily

Heffner toilet-side SEE she was proud of him   pimped-out late night

                absent father platinum   [[][absent mother's live-in brother
                presence
                mama's French roll
coif coif coif   ] 13 years old

        we ride notches in the fence
    (my board a bay
        who don't need a giddy up)

                only her pony eats oats

our begging even
            ] after [before [Halloween   [[[No clothes to wear
                                                    ] No anywhere

[] outfits for redress
[hard day's night working—dogged
] hedge clippings

Last Supper: Pigweed

1983]

WASECA, MN "Farming 2000"[weed]

pigweed paste so protein it's a whole hog
Punjab scientist begs pork kings to quit
hand-mating boars, puts his hands together
bows, prays, *please.* Pork kings won't
stomach song of their own uselessness
they keep time with the hinge on their prize
sow's pen—steel saying: *open me close me*
pork king hears *feed corn not seed corn feed*
pork queen wants pigskin roses at coronation
Punjab scientist transplants roadside weeds
his garden soil sings: *nutrients not nitrogen*
his centrifuge spins: *evidence evidence*

[1883

DATURA, NM "Gardens of Dunes"[read]

Sister Salt says Grandpa Snake said: Sand
Lizard planted amaranth. Salt shows stone
for grinding. We stop arguing near plants.
Salt names the colors. Indigo, though small,
reseeds. Salt lets her eyes sing: *bird green,*
blossom orange, moss green, blossom
yellow, white. Salt lets Indigo name each
Bushy, Fatty, Skinny, Shorty… refuge
from the boot print shod horse soldiers.
The Indian police in the old garden: new
orders. Salt buries coal near shallows—
planting like saving refuse, seeding family.

weed "Farming 2000" for *Agri News* in Rochester, MN. 1983.

read Extrapolated from Leslie Marmon Silko's *Gardens in the Dunes* (New York: Scribner, 2000:15).

Homemaking Myth: Humanitarian Aid

Jan. 2004

All year she herded up sewing machines:
Singers crated for Jakarta's Mormon
tailors. Mechanized needles sit stateside
in need of a forklift; she'd have to pay
500 bucks per foot pedal to give the gifts.
She'd hoped to bribe with bobbins,
to thread her life patterns into theirs
(the way her maid mama taught her to
cheat seam allowance to gain material).

Jan. 2005

A rewritten coastline has her packing
toothbrushes, underwear, antiseptic salve.
An assembly line, they make hygiene kits
(she and those who have no clean clothes,
no rags for tourniquets, no teeth to brush).
Perishables sit on tarmac in need of a fork-
lift, a truck, a road. She is every woman
in need of mud solid enough for a runway,
those flying lessons her papa never offered,
his homemade prop plane, his guts-n-gear.

May

8 May 1546

Reverend Lord Vicar-General[?] ordered the offending
weevils (a colony of "creepers") to pay their tithe
without delay to make three processions
around the vineyards in which they had feasted.

Having escaped excommunication, the beetles left
before, we think, completing their required devotion.
So we (with pitchfork and prayer) tromped clockwise
1, 2, 3 times round the grapes singing *mercy mercy.*

10 May 1979

To this day our hounds round the worn path with us.
The youngest son of the oldest man leafs out: green
face, green hands, foliage from his mouth. We toast
1, 2, 3 times round the grapes singing *merci merci.*

We take turns being Reverend Lord Vicar-General.
If a bee light on your arm, you're to do his homing
dance, circle your own footsteps (1, 2, 3) decrying,
for God himself, the right of all creatures to consume.

8 May 2525

To produce a vision of our past, we trace beetle paths
in bark. Yes, there're still trees. Pheromone planning
controls the pests. We keep our best vines secreted
away from those still bent on Mars. Foliage abounds

from each corner of her mouth. The middle of three
daughters leads the parade: 1, 2, 3 times round home.
Lording the particular over the general, we manage
reverence by singing mercy. Pitch forks tuning us.

[2] If it wasn't Reverend Lord Vicar-General, it was someone like him.
See page ix of Luc Ferry's *Ecological Order* (U. of Chicago Press, 1992:xi).

first food] [bitterroot

Who said "Let your silver hair down"
    Spirit bird's rose wing:[long ago]
Who said "Bitter is better"
    Dogwood digging stick:
Who said "Thanks & thanks again"
    The raided, the traded?
When wheel spoke "return,"

We disband Woolworth-pot-n-pan.[1933]
    Pitch tipis
When gunny sack said "Come May
    gather fullness."
We turn flour sacks inside out
    let Mission[1880]
BEST kiss our roots again again.

transplant] [sugarbeet

When capillary said "Action,"
    Parenchyma pulped up.
When pectin called "Close up,"
    Megaspore mother cell
Said: "Move, daughter nuclei."
    To cool late summers,
Kettle said: "Up production."

Shovels said: "More for Barceros."
    Sugar shouts: "Stop
rations." German POWs[1945] bake
    each guard a cake
& Ore Daddy Daly's horse[1893]
    gets preserved:
finest of sugar cubes in reserve.

^{long ago} "A grandmother, worrying [about her tribe's starvation]… went to the mountains…[to ask] the Creator for help…. She sat down and untied her gray hair. As she wept, her tears fell on the ground and turned into bitterroot." Told by Joanne Bigcrane in *Sacred Encounters* (U of Oklahoma Press, 1993:6).

[1933] "The culture of the Salish is passing, along with the grand old men, whose descendants are not content to be Men Without Machines." Harry Turney-High in Jerry DeSanto's *Bitterroot* (Babb, MT: Lere Press, 1996:9).

[1945] "The beet labor problem for the Bitter Root valley appears to be approaching a solution… a total of 406 prisoners located here in the valley will be used in the beet harvesting work. This labor is replacing Mexican nationals… the Coughenour store, has been refitted for a prison camp… wire fences and guard towers, and shower baths for the enlisted men guards, have been arranged" (*Northwest Tribune,* October 11, 1945).

[1893] "A race was set up for the two horses… 'If Tammany beats Lamplighter,' Copper Baron Marcus Daly said, 'I'll build him a castle.' Tammany won by 4 lengths" (www.dalymansion.org/tammany.htm).

[1880] "BEST" flour from St. Ignatius Mission, Montana. "The flour mill and mission farm also served as models of an American work ethic for Salish to emulate" (*Sacred Encounters,* U of Oklahoma Press, 1993:142).

The Plant Poems

Katie Kemple

Radiator

A steel plant with tubular runners
under floor, they surface in seven
silvery heat-hissing, gurgling stalks.
Like the cacti they need never
be watered. And, unlike most house
plants, these hibernate in Spring.
Good for those who catch cold
easily. They emit no pollen and
prefer to stand by the window.
Note: no growth ever, neither do
they move. Some say this genus
is dumb as potatoes (don't believe
everything everyone says—).
They are lovable, harmless, and
nearly impossible to kill.

Air Popper

Once populous and ubiquitous, recently
plummeting numbers have placed it on the
endangered species list. It can be identified
by the enlarged yellow and often transparent
bloom-head. Euphoric fits of pollination
send white flowerlets zooming up from
pistons in a rage of springtime ecstasy!
The flowerlets—a delectable, light and airy
food—may themselves be the cause of
decreasing populations. Gene splicing has
allowed farmers to artificially manufacture
them in air tight bags. Though not as tasty,
many have opted for this cheap and easy
stand in. Don't be fooled by the masses!
Make your home a safe habitat for this
smart, passionate, and lovely companion.

Toaster

Its leaves pop open out of heat beds
at dawn. The edible "slices" bloom
in unique varieties, ranging from rye to
pumpernickel, wheat, and an American
white. Some strains have been cultivated
to produce waffles as well as others
particular to the "breakfast pastry" family.
Over-ripe leaves may take on a blackened
appearance and burnt aroma: these
should be plucked off and never ingested.
Signs of under-ripe leaves, on the other
hand, may indicate an unhealthy plant.
Rid pot of any crushed debris that crumb
too close to roots (a dirty pot has been
known to cause premature aging in
some species). Indigenous to tropical
regions, crops can be reaped year round!
There are at least fifty charming cultivars
to choose from, but then that is why there
are whole books that cover this one plant.

Standing Fan

Placed in the "caged bird" family
for their circular barring leaves,
interior bird hum, and wing-like
rotating, inner tepals;
they typically stay active during
the summer months when petals
bloom into a "whirring rose." No
vase required, their hollow plastic
stem stands sturdy on its own.
A monstrously efficient monocotyledon,
they produce only one flower per life-
time (highly stubborn, won't move
without proper nutrients). Lacking
fragrance, they do produce
wind. Frigid heat mongers do
not make good owners! They like
electricity, and if fed amply,
can live a happy, productive life.

Desk Lamp

Several factors make this the number one
species for offices and, obviously, desks.
Most forthright—light. The luminous bulb
is protected by the petals of her flower,
which can take on any assortment of
colors from pinks and purples, to the
more workplace common blacks and
coppers. This diverse family has a range
of common forms. From hinging stems
that clamp—technically dubbed "crotch
dwellers" for their dependency on the
mechanical support of a desk—
to a potted medley, whose petals are soft
and flowers cover bulbs rested on a
dwarfed stem. The plant's most stunning
feature, however, is the bulb itself.
Devoid of bulb, they look terribly mopey.
American myth hails this the plant of
knowledge. No owner would dispute it.
Conserve bulbs by lighting only eight to
twelve hours a day, then let them "sleep."
Deceased bulbs can be replaced.

Coffee Pot

This exotic rain forest lovely employs
an unusual, somewhat backwards
method of nutrient absorption.
Soil is cradled in the petals of the
delicate *filter flower*, which drips a
dark, bitter nectar into the glass-domed
pot below. Though charming, this flower
is short-lived and must be replaced
daily. Most supermarkets carry
a surplus, but be sure to purchase
the correct size and shape! An inadequate
flower will cause silting—resulting in the
passage of "grinds" into the pot.
Soil also must be changed, and comes
in a plethora of flavors based on region,
from Brazilian to French. Less potent
formulas are available in the chemically
altered *decaffeinated* state. It's advised
that those with addictive personalities
avoid ownership. The nectar is highly
habit-forming, and can lead to yellowed
teeth, bad breath, and a jittery temperament.
Despite these negative side effects, it
remains highly populous. It should also
be noted, that though nectar is easily
purchased, and entire restaurants specialize
in its production, there is nothing quite like
brewing your own. In fact, many have
developed warm, almost intimate,
relationships with this particular group.

Carpet

Often considered the lazy man's choice,
no house should be without one. In fact,
many houses contain a variety that go
unnoticed, and underappreciated—after
all, well weeded and kept they complement
even the dullest of rooms. Whimsical
owners boast of moonlit frolics bare foot,
or setting up picnic on a fire side bed
of *circular shag*. A certain Zen quality
allows them to blend easily into most any
environment. They also come in a variety
of sizes, textures and colors, from the wide
spread *four wall creeper* to the tiny,
moisture dependent, wash room "mat."
Watering is infrequent and rarely a concern.
Mobile types take a spin toss monthly,
while grounded species prefer to be
watered in place (movement can "shock"
the plant). There are many agencies
that will do an annual watering for you.
Though it's possible to propagate from
seed, most prefer to buy by the square foot.
Your house will never look barren again!

The String Witness

from How We Came to Wear Our Bodies

Christopher Fritton

that was the year
the yarn rain started.

our blood became string.

they told us everything was string
and we believed them.

as the yarn rain fell,
          puddles accumulated.

   likewise, our blood.
then,
        our spit.

   with jute-packed cheeks,
strands of weather escaped our mouths.

                embroidered the quiet.

we had always thought that we were puddles

of cloth

but now we knew for sure.

accumulation makes one dimension three
                                or more.
apparently.   our dimensions accumulate.

we're knit.

apparently it's a simple case of direction.

the way strings move.

apparently i'm an accumulation of
dimensions in motion.

this means motion makes mass.
this means dimensions are cloth.
this means puddles are the same as

blood.

but puddles don't have a direction.

they vibrate.

they have directions.
                    i'm vibrating faster.
they told me that's why i don't look like the rain.

velocity is the only thing
that insures that
my puddle doesn't look like rain.

if i stopped vibrating. if i didn't.
i wouldn't be.

even the most massless I is made of motion.

    i am massless. light is massless.
   light is string surging.
light is lace with sewn edges.

    surged.
          i am wrapped. a surged

massless with edges made of light.

I is filamental.
you are filaments.

faster or slower.

why strings?

because nothing else could.

this is about the proportion
of thread to space in a given;
i'm the appearance of resonance
arriving by chance up against the
seams of another kind of
cloth,

another kind of light.
my velocity makes seams. laced boundaries.

i can't tell you that we're different
                             speeds
and make you understand.

                i just.

i'm showing you.

          now.

              and now.

when the yarn rain stopped,

bodies were just cloth we wore.

it didn't take long to realize we could wear
other bodies.

the soft suit they called it.

elaborate stitching patterns were made to hold
worn bodies together.

our own, and others.

the dead became fabric.

i was wearing myself out, they said.

i would be worn.

this is the story
we're told.

of how we came to wear our bodies.

body science limitation 0.0 – 0.6.7.11
Shades drawn
Moon Song
Friends

Eric Gelsinger

Inside dark apartments, hands slide along
Walls, then lose touch, inside.
I'm stuck
In body clod,
Receding from skin-clay, groping toward a hollow center.
      I don't care about my hair all messy
      I don't care about my skin kinda dirty.

I get down on my knees to plug in the light.
I'm silent. Concentrate on the socket,
Want a way out to the sky, thumb the head of the plug, push inside.
I pray for imperfect escape without whispering, sit and roll a cigarette with ritual finesse.

I light up, stumble onto the porch. It's nice, but it's so near so dear:
I could not pay the price for less;

I stand outside, smoke,
View the sky between telephone poles,
Between roof-top antennae. My weight upon a surface of a hole, cold
Glass, wall, glass, I can't go in there's nothing in.
Behind their windows, neighbors made of wind; bodies, signals,
Cohesive when a spotlight hits them prancing down the stairs.
The stars inside the telephone burn out. I walk inside, someone picks up, but no one's at
The other end.

Shades drawn

The phone rings out of darkness like out of glass,
A neurotic knell from ringing dawn.

Gnomonic 6:16 mnemonic
Shadow
Sunslant
Cthel phone,
Giant window to look from:
Reflection in glass: *egoviaradio*
Toward eretic alarm, Nawling further
From this wireriver, this morning
Too tired, last night wanted white woods' mind,
Single voice in a bilating Mouth,
Underground's submoonymous once New York numina, noctisnaut rivering,
Light leaping, skipping on the river of the wire of this woken mind
Out this city open mouth wide for wind, woods four frames give way to one wall for open
My mouth breath no interpiercing theater-flesh mandream answer.

Moon Song

I refuse to pee inside.
I won't retreat to smaller smaller spaces
Pass through door after door in order to get naked in the corner of the corner.
I'll piss under God's sky,
Lift my white eyes to the white moon, make eye contact, spit,
Micturate, split, get high, white-owl, Cliff Smith.
Live life to the fullest, fill it up again in three days, escape scandal and perdition,
Learn morphology of phonemes across proto indo-european.

Friends

There's something special this night, I feel the light that's always on me turned up so that everyone can see. Whitebodying my gruesome body, under the god-famous sky that is all streets at once. Delevan Ave, no matter where I cross, a thousand eyes that are really one, fixed on every clothed and unclothed human body, all the ones I can see Along Niagara St, all the warehouses and turn-of-the-century restaurants feel like the name of god's spelled twice from worn and burned out letters, so stopped in time to be alone so late after late-lonely nights of work. Friends on the other side of phonewalls, scotch to drink, and love to make—that's the big one—allow me—o this light quickens what it hits—not like the flashes at premiers, not like the winter moon amplified to blinding like night construction floodlights on the interstate I feel light through my body, even in the shadows where my feet tap pedals, a light that wakens me, sleeves off shirtless tucked in dashboard, windshield, gearshift. It never fails to feel to fill me all, toes in the shower, fingernails while I sleep I love this luminosity we can't escape—like on the Niagara gorge of darkness, field lights illuminating as a water muscle flexions over lip into the mist and roar and colored light. Above, the atramentous bottomless dark forever home and lights on in the kitchen to the living room: Aaron's car outside means he's inside, with maybe Damian, or Jay, or Ben, and Chelsea sure, we all are burning burning softly—softly, maybe brighter this night we together my mind reeling can't wait to get inside my body feeling something strange like death or life.

Hand to My Mouth to Help a Thought
A Manycolored Seaandsky
Toward Unpunctuated Spring

Occultatio for Early Autumn
for Mid-Winter

Jacqueline Lyons

Hand to My Mouth to Help a Thought

Before I noticed how

       I moved   hips first   then
                  shoulders neck eyes

Before I could wink   I blinked emphatically

      movement   a dark matter
          loosening gravity

I am headed   in a direction   on foot

Me + Sun
          my larger-than-life Sun-down Shadow

I teach my left hand
           and investigate walking backwards

More careful of my hands than feet
     as if the latter belonged   to some other mammal

     and painting toe nails
        mating-season pink   end-of-hibernation orange

Is it worse to notice wrongly   or not notice at all

When someone on the bus puked I wanted to puke too
     old habit of having eaten fruit from the same tree

Not telling but turning toward   looking at the hiding place

     chin trembles before the eyes begin to leak

The woman on the nightly news, purse strap pressed into her shoulder

    I knew just how she felt

        too concentrated to be kept aloft by trees any longer
        strongest pull in a single dimension

I practice steady shoulders and heartbeat
    during phone ring door slam

I changed my name to something I would turn toward when I heard it spoken

We try to slow falling by flailing   and wishing

An old man afoot, hips lost inside his overcoat, turns   shoulders neck eyes

    "Are you looking for me?"

   which part of the question
          to move toward first.

A Manycolored Seaandsky

I started in early summer
            on the shape of things

    Air has no shape. You cannot see air.

Beaded curtains, air conditioning
                    a christening drip   when entering
        blurred: coffee-ing, jellyfish-ly, marble-ation

        tearing freely through the clouds

Salt air gave me super vision of thin edges
        eyelash, ear curl, pant crease
        bubbles in a young green wine

        tiny yogurt drink containers where streets are narrowest
        every restaurant table clinking with separate glasses

Towns I slept in on the shore
        had the shape of spilled water
        and wanted the sea

One bed I tried —like lying on a cloud—
                                    a cloud!

        breathing part water/part air
        humid the thick that brushed my skin

Ancient potters there sculpted handles in a holy shape

        rooms' marble corners unworn

Semi-precious stones
        gray on the faraway beach
        up close in color
                orbiting with light

Waves came in bobbing with rocks
                in twos and threes
        improbable

I moved through the water swimmingly
        possibly patterned

        a jellyfish swam neurotoxinly
                in scattering pattern

        milky white and the shape of reflecting light

A toothy fish, sharp dentata in a soft pink mouth
        gulping air   just a hair, just one breath above sea level

        I could see it from so far away

        salt stinging my mouth as I breathed through

& the rocks not rocks, pumice—
                                porous, volcanic

        rounded   that is, circular   with depth.

Toward Unpunctuated Spring

My best young ideas   others re-mind me
                                (no one does that)

Too much or   too little tradition
        half-assed Easter egg hunt

        Spring's Time adjusted
                (good (after) morning)
                a later scarlet sunrise

At softball games   I refuse

        the chants   fake ice cream   hypnotic

        locate my   self
                within the night sky

        aerial view reveals us   heads knees elbows

                (kinds of) stars

Spring is   (choose three)

        messysexual   unevenunfurling

                unpunctuated mud and pollen

I want more than one imagination
                        to get lost among the grass(es) green(s)

        chill around the ankles while the face sunburns

                                        while lilacs and constellations spill
                from mud and lower stars

Occultatio for Early Autumn

I won't begin to tell you
how the rain went on and on,
one steel-gray twilight
into steel-black night,
am unable to explain
how mornings, dull-
nosed, reached not even
the bed, window, yard
but cruised, heavy, circling
the murky valley of downtown, blind.

I won't try to record
every sound in its wet version
not enough time to tell
of every leaf as pouting lip
drenched and dripping
nor of the *shhhr* of black tires
unpeeling rain from road
nor of brick rivulets tripping
and falling over each other,
none of the countless plinks,
plips, plups, blips of rain hitting
car hood, plastic pool, tarp,
bare branch, iron railing,
rain gutter, garden mulch.

I have no words
for the way rain glazes sound
as it enters ears, infiltrates voice
or how it smudges the line
between skin and air
between ocean and horizon;

we think we've spoken
when we've only thought.

I can not relate
how the indoors filled
with people eyeing each other
as if they'd bumped, touched,
brushed elbows, even though
they stood apart.

for Mid-Winter

What can I say about December snow
that came every third day
fresh at first then lying
in dirty layers, pressed into ice,
erasing evidence.

I want to talk about a squirrel
whose tree trunk-branch-rooftop path
I watched all fall and into winter,
layers of house it chewed through
and hundreds of chestnuts stashed,
crumbling pyramids I discovered
in closets and corners and,
in January, tossed out.

The incongruity of a herd of deer
downtown, fur next to cement,
antlered silhouettes against neon,
cannot be captured.
Their hoof prints and scat piles
opened the city,
thud and scrape invaded.

Can I describe the redemption
of an Italian deli open on Sundays,
romano, prosciutto, provolone and olives

or the diffused lavender
of snow-laden sky floating up
all that weighs heavily

or ice spirals woven by freeze and thaw
into a chain link fence
a translucent, breakable weave
to make the metal fence
temporary, beautiful.

Who Makes Their Own Language
They Want to Convert the American Finishing Company
Real Life
6 Notes for the Afterlife
Taps

John Cotter

Who Makes Their Own Language

        O, they'll blow us
wide open
       my wee moa;

that drift of sounds,
       I coo unique
as a Labrador duck

       will fly from us.
Who makes their own
       language burns maps

like Arawaks
       who mine
pure gold.

       Who makes
their own language
       falls

through a trap
       door,
joins the choir.

They Want to Convert the American Finishing Company

While your poison colors
      streaked the river
Norwich ate hearty,
      woke up early.

Kids grown hard on oatmeal
      made the life of you,
hard to think you were real
      as you are for me.

Empty city:
      old world gone under brick;
our brochures larder you with art:
      velvet heirloom, river naked.

I strain my edge
      to feel you emptier,
refuse to learn
      how real you were.

Our ties moved south
      with the labor. Your bare halls
stretch the past,
      scrub the future.

Real Life

No one from your real life stayed at home
tonight; keep up your search
for the real street
where they rack suits
your size,

the real house
where they know
your intimacies;

remember the smell of food
wholesome opium
coming out of the kitchen
children who shut doors
silently;
your shelves full of pricy frames.

You take one down,
strange as
what's behind those
vanished blinds,
you find in pages,
yellowed gold.

Study deep
as though you were
in a public library

closing early
for summer hours.

1. In the Afterlife

After that stripping
     you'll arrive bare
of the bark & warp
     of dark inertia

that clouded even the sweetest dinner
     with Jaime, say, and her Chihuahua,
aged gouda, landmines of salt, fish
     with crisp skin, Korean beer.

     Without the traffic you could hear cicadas—

       think of the nights
you've pressed against
       your girl
and still unsatisfied
you press her to the wall
       the afterlife
is like that want
       fulfilled

3. Intentions Grow Exact

I've been writing a book
about the past since High School

as the moon grows full
my arm and shoulder mire in muck

4. Stare at the Mirror, Pull Your Lips Back

It isn't that exactly

5. It Isn't Like This Life

fights with the family at table
killing time
in a record store
because you killed it
there
ten years ago

figuring out which girl's
playing air cello
on the *Esquire* cover,
eating somewhere
because at least
you know what they offer

calling the girl
you fought with
last night because
you loved her
last year

checking your messages

6. In the Afterlife

you walk away and here we are
and the one who is you isn't there

Taps

Again, taps,
5 pm:

cars at lights
quit gears, I stand

to salute
as the day dies.

Alive at home
you calm,

laughing
through

stories
already

blown up
about the kids.

for Col. A.E. Cotter (1915 – 2006)

Prose Poems

and:

Maybe...
Remembrance...

Jeff Paris

These art frames show the layers beneath the paint. This one, newspaper from 1957. This, studs of wood and lonely brass piping. The last is my favorite, gilded with gold-like paint, that I call "Mouse Highway." Stand still, study it, and you will see what I mean.

Think how it used to feel, stepping into a telephone booth, pulling the door shut, knowing each moment you spoke was consuming the quarter you fed it. You wouldn't say, "No reason, just calling…" unless you really meant, "I can't tell you how empty the street is. I have come to this box to enclose myself in your voice. To make the world through the glass a silent picture, and human sound its humming portent. I remember now. I remember how it felt for you to hold me."

On the subway this morning everyone has cellos instead of shoulder bags. Some women violins instead of purses. And, of course, heading to the airport, the upright bass on its one wheel. Lost in thought they all hold bows, incorrectly, chuffing them against the strings as the car rocks on its way. No one in tune except the twins in their stroller, boys, wailing on their pochette fiddles like angels being squeezed in a vise.

My desire for this plate of pasta is both carnal and philo-
sophical. Maybe it's the candlelight, and only my hunger for
company. Anyway, it is too hot to eat just yet. And wait…
seems to be getting hotter… Yes, the cheese is doing this
little dance, and (damn!) my fork, resting in the sauce, is
now too hot to hold. The mushrooms, become leathery
foolscaps, scud around the marinara like an anarchic pod
of whales. The penne begin to chug like loose pistons, roil-
ing flecks of spice to the surface, slimming and hardening
like bone. And without flame or audible boiling the entire
meal is shortly a dark crust rimming a white dish. I pay the
bill. It would be my word against… everything.

Between each stanza of your poem, uncannily, the lights
on the train go out. As if every five lines the world blanks,
and all that exists is the memory of what I just consumed.
Then the fan cuts in, and with a sigh, it resumes. An exag-
geration of the space you intended; but soothing, natural,
as if existence blinks for me, or as if I am transported to
the quiet place a poem goes inside us.

That stain spreading on the ceiling is actually ants. When you see it, you are not sure if reality has broken or not. If not, once you flee the ants, the fire department and some government agency will clean up and explain the whole thing. By this time next week your friends will be tired of the story, and you'll be arguing with an insurance company. If broken, the windows will be dark with them —you'll wrap curtains around their rod for a torch, and clear your way into a world gone shapeless and black.

Another fresco hidden by ocean. A scalloped column turns in kelp. The blunt chainsaw of waves guntle rocks into submission. Water teaches a patience that slowly destroys what is waited for. Add miles of ocean to anywhere, and it becomes remote.

Your parents were better lovers than you. Back when their bodies were vigorous and they were unafraid of discomfort. They had nights, such nights as you should be lucky to ever approach. I think they are embarrassed by it now. Perhaps it is this embarrassment that has infected your own attempts. Or just the nagging sense that it could all be better. And so this, this is the mystery you've been beating up against all these years. I must say… you're taking it very well.

Dog chasing sun and moon. Ocean tumbling after. Its breakers filled with lutes and lyres. Each crested swell beyond, a woman's stomach. She is meditating. Of her navel, I am sitting in its boat. Stars unveil above like my foot falling asleep. In the lull, they burn white, then blue, then red. An unseen finger ashes each in turn.

I'm not afraid to say angels are battered white helicopters hiding against clouds or in shafts of sun. That their muffled whump whump whump is easily mistaken for your heart thudding through your veins, as they only hover near in moments of crises, mundane or epic: the teetering glass of milk, the hospital discovering anthrax, her hand wandering up my thigh.

Maybe this evening over me
is a tonnage
in a netting, creaking westward
by some heavenly crane.

It has never fallen
and no doubt never will
but I feel its sway like
a weight in my sinuses
its heavy pass
a slow gasp in my ears.

A stroll beneath this overwhelming assembly
means I lean
when it leans,
the breath in me
at the mercy
of its infinitesimal dip and rise.

To be sad here
is a small thing
where all things are small.
Is to be a dot
tracing sidewalks
like a burning fuse
of the softest hiss.

Remembrance. As if each day is a shell
I abandon for a slightly smaller one.
Around which sunlight foams from deep above
and a moment dribbles in one granular syllable,
scouring a shiny "etch" down the wall.
There's probably more where that
came from. Something must account for every
bit of pearl the world contains. Nothing
can happen on its own.

As Touching the Shell
Bicarbonate of Signage
Simply Dork It
Is What It Is
Non-Recidivist Lyric
Somewhere in Oregon
Things Made from Coconut
Unaccredited Joules

Michael Ives

As Touching the Shell

Swift currents of pages
pass between the banks
of the river, an autonomous

zone legible under floodlights.
Hordes flow into it
who think themselves

trinkets thrown among huge
bargaining shadows, a
special form of petition,

perfected in stillness,
if no one near is around.
In adult form it eats

almost nothing. Arrows
yawn within, thinking to build
the last object you shall see,

which always believes
you, against the advice
of the decoding jewel.

Bicarbonate of Signage

Sipping bisque near
the helmet feeder: modern
equivalent to a broose,

or race to the bridegroom's
residence for bourbon
and pliant slag.

Peculiarly too,
because skid-
product blowback

falsifies colon *You!*
will "blintz" here
for 5 minutes

at most
salvaged among
her interviews

with *mantid* community
a severe cupping colon *Get
your stuff* and… Zodiac

of total recklessness
while handling RV
enters house

of
painful childbirth colon science
of.

Simply Dork It

Crap singing
itself into
spatio-phemeral

mood soak
(oh
very leek a booby

bane) across
octaves
in accordance

with micro-structural
whethering minus
antique heart

attack-like
deployment of
idiot caliber

-ization, or walk,
as such—skew-graph
more a linkwork—into

harms' arms.
People: listen
and believe.

Is What It Is

The peen-
veldted alloy
of my head

and another
constant
is what it is,

is maybe torn
from an infarct
in Toulouse

again, maybe. Withal
her face = thirteenth
tire bomb

but once in
this dale
of English

and ascendant
Manx
variables,

which push/
pushed my
patience into

the open until
it squealed
in its

discursive "Jacque"
to these wilds,
briefly.

Non-recidivist Lyric

Dirty talk and coogirl
portamentos—they
bring to mind

the fatal carjacking,
then drift apart, then
reconnoiter

in the word
"hour." One
wants gun metal

thighs introduced
where late a
dope concordance

among pronouns
had left the house party
feeling like many manic

fountains, or many
manic fountains-ish, but
shall nevermore

gush, nor
break through
the turbulent prefab

of this corrected
self, dune-like
and alone.

Somewhere in Oregon

Forcing all memory of my dear Patroclus
Between thermo-seal plates, the eviction
Synched up with

I had wanted to prove it using an airbag
Last name of Siefert
He repeated, though because his tongue but lightly grazed the velar ridge

Naturally I thought he was saying *sea fur*
Was removed to a partial knowledge
Of these coasts

Things Made from Coconut

An unrealistic surface
to volume ratio
nucleating

the gnat swarms
are an example, and
controlled fades,

and words
for that *pop!*
an animal's bladder

makes, softly,
nonexistent-
ly, as in "the bite of the crane

fly" (or as the wisdom
literature terms it, "the
bite of the bite

of the crane
fly), nonetheless
it commandeth recalcitrant

spooge along
the gunwales
to dissolve.

With a spruce mallet
you must flatten
this last macaroon.

Unaccredited Joules

No surprise I've
chosen not to reinvade
yesterday's duchy

of bad breath.
Weekends yanked up
into torso

of alienated labor
like a retracting
testicle. The old

church modes:
human, world, sky—you
just can't park them

here anymore.
I plant a begonia
in the bell

of an old trumpet,
stack some catalogues
around it, ostensibly—

give succor
to an asterisk
posing as a beach.

Graffiti
Barrenshe
The Making of Thomas Sweeney
Port Wine, Portcullis

Jaime Corbacho

Graffiti

For you, dear, a palace
with a thin pate of cloud.
I have built it abandoned,
tuned to abandon's wet howl.
Its girth razed to tinder reads
Jose loves Yosema.

For you, love, six stories
of cave dust, of wire bent
to arms; where snap cans pasa
doble foils of Muriel
cigars to the tinny chords
Jose loves Yosema.

For you, sweet, this shadow
box, the end of the block.
You can fill it with secrets
or locks of your hair or for-
tunes inside eggshells hiding
Jose loves Yosema.

For you, lark, this Odin,
this Gladsheim sky father.
Empty as whistles, lonely
as steel, you must rattle in-
side him, teach him new words like
Jose loves Yosema.

For you, belle, this building.
Come quiet. Watch your step.
This mattress Medusa springs
coils from her head. I lay you
on sawdust, on whispers of
Jose loves Yosema.

For you, my Yosema,
my name and my word. What
once was a factory now
charred to three words. It's destruc-
tion's strange paradise love's lit-
ter on tombs. It is spray bright.

It is paint truth.
Jose loves you.

Barrenshe

This valley is full of killing wombs,
tiny succulents like bleached lettuce.
This jade plant was the only thing
she could keep alive.
They say
when the Earth tilts
like
this
women become pregnant with
reckless abandon.

There are terrible secrets in this desert.
A child is the compass of every dream
she bled through.

So goes, his name was Sand
and he wanted a boy.
To make boys one must
slip the knot
from a Claddagh of grass.
To make sand one must
lap rain
into a casually drawn orifice.

In the paste heat, swooping
low, he picked her carcass
of daylight and lesser evils.

To sin without reckoning,
he could not but break
a meal with his beak
before,
unfit

for God,
she buried them like water.
More salt than eyes could ferry
their shifting quietus
to pallbearers who'd
run out of things to play with.

A tremor in the sand
mines little ones
spitting forks like snakes
A barely disturbed sign of their unbecoming.
There's a maze in here, somewheres,
we've had to sew around.
A blossomless stem of blood
trailing from her watercolours
this mirage of empty
pulse
points.
Steams the earth where sent
her boys.

Forgiveness
bears the sun on its back
like a mute amulet.

She will carry her heart
large
for the taking. She
will map the valley
in blood like cold-
filtered light from red planets.
She will lay down
a sigh
that ends with no faces

and loosen her skirts
for the taking
up of souls.

The Making of Thomas Sweeney

Fortunate for the lightning
the trees were tall and full-derbied,
it caught in their brims
with a smart dash of pheasantry.

Thomas S-s-sweeney
with his st-st-stutter
saw it all from the inside.
Trapped in the millinery
with Montmort to his chest.

In the parlor trick of storm,
when hats were swapped
surreptitiously side to side,
even the heavens couldn't wager

under which tree hid the boy,
under which tree stood the man.

Port Wine, Portcullis

1.
When the grapes were large enough to catch
the rain in tarns between their green cheeks,
we were allowed to pinch them
from the vine.

Grandpa trained them up
the bit of portcullis nicked from a castle that
pantomimed death for an audience of soldiers.
As in life, the gate survived.

2.
Symbiotically attaching history
to the fruit,
the grapes grew oblong and sour.

Filling my mouth, I would dream of
mongrel kings, of siege, of treason,
hanging its own fruit from the gallows.

3.
He would have a glass of port in his study
after most meals, requiring the sweetness,
the time alone.

The loneliness of others drew slack, pooled
thick in the belly of the empty glass. When
he'd leave, I sneak in, wet my little fingers
in it. Drunk off the residue.

4.
On schoolwork pretense, I was once
invited in the study to talk about war.

He told me how he swam the English
Channel after his ship was attacked, and as
though he couldn't stop swimming, told
me of lust, bastards in other countries,
of death that came slowly, ineptly,
dragging incarnadine trails back to the barracks.

5.
When I think of him, I think of those
grapes climbing the portcullis. How I turned
them over and over in my chubby
fingers before eating them.
The bitter beckoning like the space
left by a missing tooth, eat them two by
two, four by four, until Grandpa yelled
from his study window, "Enough!
You'll be sick!"

Matthew Klane

90° N – 180° W

The- Contour of Our Soul

the- torrential rolling sound

the- shi'ah ayatollahs-

"the- men who run Tehran"

45° N – 180° W

The- Terra Incognita

has no earthly analogue

as no theatre

thresholds duodenum'

no number can warm the- doldrums

0° N – 180° W

90° N – 135° W

The- Front

to and fro' come and went

radioed cicada staccato-

"the- air is wearing a wire"

45° N – 135° W

The- Cleric's Guerra - They Were The-

thunder (G-d on the- ground)

their firearms were filament'

their bodies' flesh clairvoyant'

light' up the- night

0° N – 135° W

90° N – 90° W

The- Subtextual Revolution

    turns surround the- severed

event' the- sea underneath

    author' dun heavy cloth her

10'000 centre fugue

45° N – 90° W

The- Deep Speaker

    his brain is a mountain range

his ears are secret caves

    his mouth' breathes in' a "b"

his mouth' breathes out' behemoth

0° N – 90° W

90° N – 45° W

The- Cub Scouts

    the- boy's club's url

"where wanton girls want to learn"

    dot

"teeth their mother's bear"

45° N – 45° W

The- Movies

    i.e. the- central govern's

dreaming coverage

    monitors every' behoove

0° N – 45° W

90° N – 0° E

The- Grand Camera

   the- crater w/in

  the- o- crater

90° N – 45° E

The- Great Satan

heaven-sent troopers swooping down

   upon the- carcasses

of sheep and goats'

   stark white trees' shattered gas

45° N – 0° E

The- Parameters

  pinpoint a military narrative

will the- people' win the- war'

  trace the- data' free the- arc

45° N – 45° E

The- News Recruits

    spin like spacemen'

disinter' misconstrue

  a pit: is a "Palestine Hotel"

"Taliban Ballet": what they call a coup

0° N – 0° E

0° N – 45° E

90° N – 90° E

The- First Report

I heard the- thud of mortar

intermittent roar

I saw the- word "ambush"

enter "into" literature

90° N – 135° E

The- English Channel

fish hits the- tent - "thwack!"

then quiet as a piece of paper

the- shape of this husht- animus

intimates a hinterworld

45° N – 90° E

The- Scud and The- Stinger

errat-attack -ack at random

that rocket there-

it's honing err-

on someone somewhere in the- city

45° N – 135° E

The- Journal Gentry's

whirlybird panorama:

straw and sand and dusty skirts'

bandanna' mud-hut' mujahadeen'

cacophony' ramshackle' yak

0° N – 90° E

0° N – 135° E

0° S — 180° W

The- Imam Age

I am the- hammer and the- anvil

I am him who

will unveil a cinema - so violent pious

it'll render the- infinite moot

45° S — 180° W

The- Deadpan Routine

    "I own this whole tone"

"rhythm and tempo"

    "I partition alien phenomena"

"then" - "empty" - "them"

90° S — 180° W

0° S — 135° W

The- Poem's Homeland

  headline-

    in between history and myth

is a little' clandestine slit-

45° S — 135° W

The- Martian Gaza

    "extra-terrestrial": more and

more devout

    "Texas kilometer": less than'

stone's throw

90° S — 135° W

0° S – 90° W

The- Thin Wind

      dis'mantles all withstanding'

thorough as theory'

      clearing the- clout forest'

thrashing the- in'ternational in'tifada

45° S – 90° W

The- Outside World - Tell Me

      how wayward wide spreads

through the- village' why

      spiraling' sprawling' splinter-

ing' spillage

90° S – 90° W

0° S – 45° W

The- I Desires

      sister - border - bone-cellar

colonizing the- soil's

      clean non-connotative dossier

45° S – 45° W

The- Meaning of Hyphen

apostrophe' quote:

      "quarantine - turmoil

map cap-size divide"

90° S – 45° W

0° S – 0° E

The- Associated Press

    dispatch death from the- dirt

"vertebrae brouhaha"

    "various cadaver splay"

there is no: safe place

45° S – 0° E

The- Elements

    limbs' distill in themselves-

they are not symbol' thought'

    spindly' lingual' silhouette-

they are not: life-like

90° S – 0° E

0° S – 45° E

The- Essence of The- Word

    the- essence of the- word "have-not"

    the- essence of the- word "fulfill"

    the- essence of the- word "warfare"

    the- essence of the- word "earshot"

45° S – 45° E

The- Air Plane

    the- cargo's fear

"certain micro-chemical skirmishes"

    dot

"very precise strife"

90° S – 45° E

0° S − 90° E

The- Third World Poor Toward

the- fourth world'

donning hard-hats' crow-bars' blow-

torches' powering

down the- price

45° S − 90° E

The- Next Person Murdered

I was rousted out of bed'

blindfolded'

led like a cow by a rope'

the- gun- to my head

90° S − 90° E

0° S − 135° E

The- Post-Modem Language

"texta firma":

encoded in a tungstate of manganese

"mottled water":

money unfroze

45° S − 135° E

The- Nouns

the- An-thro-po-cene sky

the- area of a square

the- contra-puntal planet

the- sun- minus one

90° S − 135° E

Each station its own gift
one part conceivable
the other not.

Then the stranger entered
the desert & crossed
& he remembered & stood under
the whole of it.

He did not find anything familiar
or useful, either on
the mountain or on the plain.

***from* Meditations on the 40 Stations of Mansour Al-Hallaj**

Pierre Joris

5. wonder ('ajab)

and you'll find
or wander if you don't
and if you do
wander to wonder

a wonder is a jab in the head
a wonder pries the heart ajar

or is a done thing too often
blinds us to what's left
to do.

so he walks on water.
whatever. a miracle in other
words is a wonder. *Ein
Wunder.*

some one sore and wounded.
a real god or wonder-
worker.

the loaves and the wine
at the wedding——a neat
trick but one we'd need

to be able to do anywhere
all the time. we can,
or could——that wonder would

be called just
distribution
of the world's wealth.

6. perishing ('atab)

he called that just
retribution
but nothing retro
is just

only life going
forward
is just even in its
perishing

'atab, to die into
the breath
that alivens
you

leaven of perishing
petite mort
or even just the dream
of it

that which only
the others
do and I do not
experience

unless it is the
perishing
into the just
breath

7. exaltation (tarab)

to gain air
is his exaltation
measurable

in inches as
tarab is not.
we do what

we can, altitude
is not attitude,
I let you know

though I have no
saving ordinance, am
not a latter day

saint, though there's
essential dignity
in the simple

way each one
of us exults his
house or this day,

raising it high
but not higher
than high.

8. avidity (sharah)

the opposite of sharing
does not invite

a city is full of it
the old country

slogan
ora et labora

has only its
rhyme scheme left

after the laughter
the fat of greed

dissolves
a charred remembrance

a *haram*
on the greedy king

of kings. if
you don't

believe go
to the avidity

primer. this is
a method

not a product.
use it with any kit.

2.
The word
crossed over

lost its moral
on the way

to the lab,
hear in it

the dissociation-
dependent strength

of any acid or base.
A protein-shark

in uncooked egg whites
hogs the biotin

we need to live
& needs bacteria, yeasts,

molds, algae,
some plant life.

Of course it can be
bottled and we

beat any lower price.
It's all in the

brand name and we've
got that sewn up.

11. comradeship (rifq)

we stand here, riffing
on comradeship

though we don't know
the first or the last

letter of it. though we are
—have to be—

in the middle of it, of
what Creeley called

the company, i.e. those
we break bread with,

eat with even if it turns
out to be poisoned

fish as we did that once—
the comradeship goes on

in the particle com links
us to the common

& a manifesto of equality
& we will keep standing

here in the wind on the corner
where desert and city meet

we will keep standing here
our hands in your pockets

always riffing even
if some of us are spectral

comrades now, as it is
exactly our job to be close

to those who are gone
to bring their news

talk their voices
we are all they have

left, squeezed as they are
in the tight fists

our hands make
in our pockets.

Moundz: Mens Mend Mons Mont Mond

Aaron Lowinger

Space in which time disappears. Space which opens up the air. I can only really think when I'm walking. I can't tell how fast time passes when I'm walking. Then I feel liquid. Inside the weather looking out.

In my country the rain is sweat. Maybe we can meet. Every night the leaves hang on trees. The smell in the Scajaquada Creek is only algae. Couldn't tell the rain from sweat. Out along the New York State Thruway. And along the lake. Cars over rainwater. I remember when I was kid in Pennsylvania. No one had any money. I'd rather feel the earth beneath my feet. My t-shirt wrapped around my CD/mp3 player. There's a tunnel through darkness. I turned the music to 'so fucking loud.' I wanted my ears to bleed water. And stay in the song.

The radio is on. The TV is on. The record player on. The lights on. The alarm clock on. The backup on. The iTunes on. The telephone on. Cars outside run. Above, the street-lights on. The TV tower blinks. The radio tower blinks. Behind them the night. And the lights holding it up. Beyond them the river. I want to wake up and then you'll tell me your middle name. Let it be Marie, Eliza or Elise. Or Jennifer.

Bright and tight. Hold down at the corners. Flour in her soul. Wires overhead. Cars by the thousands. Can't tell if it's snow, rain, or sunlight on my hat. Where I live. The city compass. The compass of a city. Beef to heels. Each house its own hell. Lying in your sweet skin smell. And you say, despite the noise of the bridge, that you're ready to follow me. You say you're ready to be whatever I need you to be. Cazenovia leans in grease stain on undershirt he cleans his glasses with. There's a highway of smoke above her shoulder. She's taking notation from God. They just can't believe this thing happening. To them. Walked onto the parade. The mountains sparkled. The sea kissed the earth.

Strong the stone mountain. To the extent that we're human and make distances. That I barely remember. But this I was told: we learned to speak on the day Joshua came out and put a stick in the ground. 'Now listen, this way up, this way down. Behind your hand. In front of your head. Back.' I see something moving.

Think I'll pack it up. Back where it suddenly gets so dark. Then the stars really shoot out. I've seen two last week. Next to church. One time watching body heat come off in the dew. Streetlight. Right foot numb. Fast as I can. I feel the way for the path. Small moon no light. Big dipper waits. It's bad for your heart. I find roof shingles on the lawn. The ave looks like a yellow tunnel. Now the leaves. The lake around. Flash. Before the railroad. I burn a lot of gas. My only ID is illegal. Living with it in my heart. I can feel flags flash off a small wind. I'm going to run all the way to Tonawanda. My brother beats me to the corner. I got a bassoon. He's got a sousaphone. I found where the Scajaquada Creek enters a six mile long tunnel from the Galleria to McKinley's grave. Next to the New York State Thruway. Then my eyes got big on the air. Between Colonial Circle and Soldiers Circle. There's a tree expanding.

Rain around the ring around the moon. Faster under the trees that look like they should
have leaves. Instead the houses. The houses stand like faces. Skin falling off everywhere.
The harder I ran. And more skin. I didn't even have money to burn. High the sky is.
One body of water. A car horn. Fewer cars than normal. Now it is night and we burn.
The lake pounds the bed. Under the moon I watch the street wave. Sirens in my head.
Nothing the burn. I burn breath. I burn heat. I make water. I burn skin. Tree to tree. A
string. Noun Verb Noun. Cats blank sidewalks. Love the night.

The sun just disappears. Serve and Protect. So blind I could not see. This week's been a blur. But I was very conscious of it happening. Lungs fill with fluid. Feeling that way ya know. Sex after church. I'm in my best. The cost has been psychic, not physic. I remember the caterpillars we found in the park along the Susquehanna. It's a chrysalis for butterflies and a cocoon for moths. Webs in the cereal. It rained. The ground didn't dry. The sun went blind but I couldn't even tell. I had a dream I owned a gun. I took it into work and shot pieces of meat and plates and fake butter jars. And the tree. I shot the tree.

The sun has nothing to do with warmth or light. When the rain turned to snow I made
it back to the house. All night in sleep while the house shook I felt her body praying
next to mine. The temple of her armpit. I was happy to have a ringing phone the morn-
ing after. It opened things up. I felt a little less fearful and closer to myself. My father
would put the radio on in every room of the house.

We have a home in the house. Mundial mouths with legs to walk. House tucked in a row. A sun blanketing the trees in HD. The river the power lines last ice in HD. I can't relax. My mouth walked away. Full of heat. Put ice cream on the river. Watched my home vanish in the current. Walked. Stopped. Jogged. Good and easy. Can't relax. My window faces west. In the late afternoon. You know what. I sleep in my head. My body stays awake. 'My heart don't pump Kool-Aid.' You know how. Like. My face covers in sweat. I see a one I know. The trees lift in HD. Little wind licks us. The power lines might be telephone lines. I think I can hear you. Blue and no shadows. Meridian. To come.

She's taking notation from God. They just can't believe this thing happening. My Tigris is the Niagara. Walked onto the parade but got caught out there in the dark. The mountains sparkled. Light poured out of every window. Cold wind in my face. Looking up at my house. My bedroom light on. It's good to be home.

Brandon Shimoda—see: *The Pines* w/ Phil Cordelli (ongoing collaborative project, 2003 – present)—see also: *POOL, Aufgabe, Cannibal, Glitterpony, the tiny, Verse, Wildlife Poetry Magazine, Xantippe, Barrow Street, New Orleans Review, TYPO Magazine*—editor of *Cutbank Magazine* (www.cutbankpoetry.blogspot.com)—curator of Missoula-based reading and performance series *New Lakes* (www.thenewlakes.blogspot.com)—online: (www.thepines.blogspot.com)—**Thom Donovan**—see: *Mantle* w/ Kyle Schlesinger (Atticus/Finch, 2005), *Tears Are These Veils* w/ Abby Walton (Wild Horses of Fire Press, 2004), *Sudden Miles* (Potes and Poets, 1999)—see also: *Antenae, Aufgabe, Combo, Cuneiform Press, Kenning, P-Queue, Fanzine*—forthcoming: essay on "Paradisical Beauty" in *Crayon*—founder and curator of the Manhattan-based events series *Peace on A*—online: (whof.blogspot.com)—**Jonathan Minton**—see: *Lost Languages* (Long Leaf Press, 1999)—see also: *Coconut, Castagraf, the Columbia Poetry Review, Free Verse*—editor of *word for/word* online journal (www.wordforword.info)—currently: teaches English at Glenville State College—**Adam Golaski**—see: *All Hallows, LVNG, Conjunctions, Supernatural Tales, Lit, American Letters & Commentary, word for/word, CutBank Poetry, McSweeney's*—see also: "Weird Furka" in the anthology *Acquainted with the Dark* (Ash-Tree Press, 2004)—co-founder and co-editor of *New Genre* (www.new-genre.com)—**Lori Anderson Moseman**—see: *Persona* (Swank Books, 2003), *Cultivating Excess* (Eighth Mountain, 1992), *Walking the Dead* (Heaven Bone, 1990)—see also: *Harpur Palate, Slab, Feile-Festa*—curator and chapbook publisher for the High Water Mark Salon series (Upper Delaware River area)—co-editor of Swank Books (www.swankwriting.com) and publications coordinator for the Upper Delaware Writers Collective—*All Steel* was written under the auspices of a PSC-CUNY grant—**Katie Kemple**—co-founder of Pop Raqs DC, a Washington DC-based expansive dance company (www.popraqs.com)—**Christopher Fritton**—see: *Diagram 6.4, Pilot, Pataphysica, Sleepingfish, name*—editor and creative controller of the assembling *Ferrum Wheel* and co-editor of Ferrum Wheel Press (www.ferrumwheel.blogspot.com)—currently: member of the sound poetry performance troupe BUFFFLUXUS—artwear project *Make Beauty* vintage ties (www.makebeauty.us)—**Eric Gelsinger**—see: *Nevertheless* (House Press, 2005), *Non Numerantur Sed Ponderantur* w/ Aaron Lowinger, Tawrin Baker, and Damian Weber (House Press, 2002), *The Following* (House Press, 2001)—see also: *Ecopoetics, Drill, string of small machines, No Tell Motel*—co-founder of House Press (www.housepress.org)—currently: works in the Alternative Liquidity Unit of D.E. Shaw & Co.—online: (www.gelsingers.blogspot.com)—**Jacqueline Lyons**—

see: *The Way They Say Yes Here* (Hanging Loose Press, 2004)—see also: *Interim, Barrow Street, Colorado Review, Florida Review, Quarter After Eight, Puerto del Sol, Sonora Review, AGNI (online), Hanging Loose*—currently: teaches literature and writing at the University of Nevada, Las Vegas—**John Cotter**—see: *3rd Bed, Hanging Loose, The Columbia Journal of American Studies, Coconut, Good Foot, Volt*—investigating publication: *Under the Small Lights* (novel)—theater: directed Girish Karnad's *Tughlaq* (Harvard University, 2006), performed in Jeff Van Dreason's *7ate9* (Boston Center of the Arts, 2006)—currently: completing a thesis on Anthony Burgess—online: (www.johncotter.net)—**Jeff Paris**—see: chapbook *The Mothskull Windchime* (2001)—co-founder and co-editor of *New Genre* (www.new-genre.com)—currently: teaches music to pre-schoolers—**Michael Ives**—see: *The External Combustion Engine* (Futurepoem Books, 2005)—see also: *Conjunctions, Octopus, 26, New Orleans Review*, and the anthology of international sound poetry *Homo Sonorus*—see also: works w/ the language/performance trio *F'loom*—currently: teaches at Bard College—**Jaime Corbacho**—see: chapbooks *Killingly* (2004) and *Tricked into Waking* (2004)—see also: *Lit, Rattapallax*—forthcoming: new short fiction "Honeymoon" in *New Genre*—studio assistant to installation artist Rachel Perry Welty—**Matthew Klane**—see: *whale Male 1-10* (Flim Forum Press, 2003), *Situation as Plan* (House Press, 2002), *The Meister-Reich Experiments* online at (www.housepress.org)—see also: *Nerve Lantern, Ambit, name, Spork, Plantarchy, string of small machines, word for/word*—forthcoming: *B______ Meditations* (Swank Books, 2007)—**Pierre Joris**—see: *Poasis* (Wesleyan University Press, 2001), *h.j.r.* (Otherwind Press, 1999)—essays: *A Nomad Poetics* (Wesleyan University Press, 2003)—translations: Paul Celan *Lightduress* (Green Integer, 2004), Pablo Picasso *The Burial of Count Orgaz & Other Poems* (Exact Change, 2004)—co-editor of *Poems for the Millennium vol. 1* and *Poems for the Millennium vol. 2* (University of California Press, 1995 and 1998)—online: (www.pierrejoris.com), (www.pjoris.blogspot.com)—**Aaron Lowinger**—see: *Open Night* (House Press, 2006), *Autobiography 1: Perfect Game* (House Press, 2005)—see also: *Spell, Drill, string of small machines*—co-founder of House Press (www.housepress.org)—online: *Moundz* is an ongoing experiment located at (www.moundz.blogspot.com) which utilizes QSL cards archived by mm cross and featured at (www.myqsl.org)—**Luke Daly**—see: *The Vandalism Questions* (House Press, 2006), *Of a Free Town* w/ Barrett Gordon (House Press, 2005)—see also: *Drill, Spell, Small Town*—co-editor of *string of small machines*—online: (www.housepress.org)—